Advanced Topics

Tables

Create relationships between tables

1. On the Database toolbar, click the Relationships button 🔡.
2. On the Database toolbar, click the Show Table button 🔄 to open the Show Table dialog box.
3. Select the desired tables, click **Add**, and click **Close**.
4. In the Relationships window, drag a field from the first table to a field in the second table. The Edit Relationships dialog box will appear.
5. Click **Join Type** to open the Join Properties dialog box. Then, select the desired option and click **OK**.
6. Check **Enforce Referential Integrity** and click **Create**.

Restrict data entry with input masks

1. Open the desired table in Design view.
2. Select the field to which you want to apply an input mask.
3. Under Field Properties, on the General tab, place the insertion point in the Input Mask box.
4. Next to the Input Mask box, click the Build button ⬚ to start the Input Mask Wizard.
5. Select the desired input mask and click **Finish**.

Input Mask:	Data Look:
Phone Number	(206) 555-1212
Social Security Number	831-86-7180
Zip Code	98052-6399
Extension	63215
Password	*******
Long Time	1:12:00 PM

   *NOTE: If you want to create a custom input mask, click **Edit List**.*
6. Close the table. When prompted to save changes, click **Yes**.

Create a table based on a query

1. Open the desired query in Design view.
2. Choose **Query**, **Make-Table Query**.
3. In the Table Name box, enter a name for the table that will be created.
4. Click **OK**.
5. On the Query Design toolbar, click the Run button ❗ to create the new table.

Improve performance through indexing

1. Open the desired table in Design view.
2. Choose **View**, **Indexes** to open the Indexes window.
3. Under Index Name, select a blank cell.
4. Enter a name for the index and press (TAB).
5. Under Field Name, from the drop-down list, select the field to be indexed, and then press (TAB).
6. Under Sort Order, from the drop-down list, select the desired option—
   Ascending or Descending.

Index Name	Field Name	Sort Order
LastName	LastName	Ascending
PostalCode	PostalCode	Ascending
PrimaryKey	EmployeeID	Ascending
IndexName	HireDate	Ascending
7. Close the Indexes window.

Online integration

Use the Page Wizard to save data in HTML format

1. In the Database window, under Objects, click **Pages**.
2. Double-click **Create data access page by using wizard**.
3. Select the desired table or query, select the desired fields, and click **Next**.
4. Add the desired grouping levels (if any) and click **Next**.
5. Set the desired sort order (if any) for each field and click **Next**.
6. Specify a page title, select **Open the page,** and click **Finish**.
7. Close the page, click **Yes**, and save the HTML file.

SQL

Manually enter a SQL statement in a query

1. In the Database window, under Objects, click **Queries**.
2. Double-click **Create query in Design view**.
3. Select the tables you want to include, click **Add**, and click **Close**.
4. Choose **View**, **SQL View**.
5. Enter the desired SQL statement.
6. Save the query.

Macros

Create a macro

1. In the Database window, under Objects, click **Macros**.
2. Click 🔲 New to open a blank Macro window.
3. Under Action, from the drop-down list, select the first action.
4. In the accompanying Comment field, enter a description for the specified action.
5. Enter the remaining actions and their descriptions.
6. Save the macro. To run it, click ❗ on the Macro Design toolbar.

Queries

Copy data between tables

1. Create a query that extracts the data you want to copy to another table. Then, open the query in Design view.
2. Choose **Query**, **Append Query** to open the Append dialog box.
3. From the Table Name list, select the table to which you want to append the extracted data, and then click **OK**.

Append To	
Table Name: Order Details	OK
⦿ Current Database	Cancel
○ Another Database:	
4. Save and run the query.

Editing

Turn error checking on or off

1. Choose **Tools**, **Options**.
2. Activate the Error Checking tab.
3. Under Settings, check or clear **Enable error checking**.
4. Under Form/Report Design Rules, set the desired options.

   NOTE: To change the color of the error indicator, use the provided drop-down list Error indicator color: �Red ▼.

View object dependencies

You can use a task pane to view dependency information for an open object or the selected object in the Database window. Here's what you do:

1. Choose **View**, **Object Dependencies** to display the Object Dependencies task pane. By default, this pane provides a list of all objects that use the selected object. This list will include all dependent tables, queries, forms, and reports.
2. Select **Objects that I depend on** to view a list of objects that are being used by the selected object.
3. To expand an object in the list, click the plus sign (+) next to the object's icon.

*NOTE: By default, hidden objects will not be displayed in the Object Dependencies task pane. To make all hidden objects visible, choose **Tools**, **Options**, activate the View tab, and check **Hidden objects**.*

Basic Topics

Database creation

Name database files and objects

Database and object names can have any combination of letters, numbers, special characters, and embedded spaces, with the following exceptions:

- Names cannot contain more than 64 characters and cannot start with a space.
- Names cannot include periods (.), exclamation points (!), accents (`), or brackets ([ ]).

NOTE: It's a good idea to use underscores (_) between words instead of spaces.

Use the Database Wizard

1. Choose **File**, **New**.
2. In the New File task pane, under Templates, click **On my computer**.
3. Activate the Databases tab, select the desired template, and click **OK**. The File New Database dialog box will appear.
4. Navigate to the desired storage location, enter a file name for the database, and click **Create**. The Database Wizard will start automatically.
5. Click **Next** and then follow the remaining steps of the wizard. You'll select fields, set styles for screen displays and reports, and specify a database title. When you're done, click **Finish**.

Tables

Create a new table

1. In the Database window, under Objects, click **Tables**.
2. Double-click **Create table in Design view**.
3. For each field you want to create, specify a field name, data type, and description. To apply additional control options, use the General tab (under Field Properties).
4. Choose **File**, **Save**, enter a name for the table, and click **OK**. If you have not defined a primary key, you will be prompted to do so.

Set a primary key

1. Open the desired table in Design view.
2. Select the row that you want to define as a primary key.
3. Do one of the following:
   - Choose **Edit**, **Primary Key**.
   - On the Edit toolbar, click ⚷.
   - Right-click the selected row and choose **Primary Key**.

   A key icon will appear next to the selected row to identify it as the primary key.

	Field Name	Data Type	Description
⚷	Last Name	Text	Candidate's last name
	First Name	Text	Candidate's first name

Records

Add a record to a table datasheet

1. In the Database window, double-click the desired table to open it in Datasheet view.
2. Select any cell in the table.
3. Choose **Insert**, **New Record** to create a new record at the bottom of the table.

   NOTE: You can also use the New Record button ▶ on the Table Datasheet toolbar.

Queries

Create a simple query

1. In the Database window, under Objects, click **Queries**.
2. Double-click **Create query by using wizard** to start the Simple Query Wizard.
3. Select the source table(s) for the query, add the desired fields, and click **Next**.

4. Enter a title for the query, select the desired option for viewing or modifying the query's design, and click **Finish**.

Manually create a query

1. In the Database window, under Objects, click **Queries**.
2. Double-click **Create query in Design view**.
3. In the Show Table dialog box, on the Tables tab, select a table, click **Add**, and click **Close**.

4. In the first cell of the Field row, use the drop-down list to select the desired field. Then, configure the desired parameters and criteria for your results.
5. Select and configure other fields as needed.
6. Choose **Query**, **Run** to test the query.
7. Save the query, or return to Design view to make changes.

Forms and reports

Use the Form Wizard to create a form

1. In the Database window, under Objects, click **Forms**.
2. Double-click **Create form by using wizard** to start the Form Wizard.
3. Select a source table and/or query, select the desired fields, and click **Next**.
   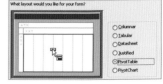
4. Select a form layout and click **Next**.
5. Select a form style and click **Next**.
6. Enter a title for the form, select the desired option for viewing or modifying the form's design, and click **Finish**.

Locate data from forms

1. In the Database window, under Objects, click **Forms**.
2. Double-click the desired form to open it in Form view.
3. Place the insertion point in the field you want to search.
4. On the Form View toolbar, click the Find button 🔍.

5. On the Find tab, in the Find What box, enter the text or value you want to find.
6. Click **Find Next**.

Use the Report Wizard to create a report

1. In the Database window, under Objects, click **Reports**.
2. Double-click **Create report by using wizard** to start the Report Wizard.
3. Select a source table, select the desired fields, and click **Next**.
4. Complete the remaining steps of the wizard. You'll select a layout and style for the report, and you'll specify a report title. When you're done, click **Finish**.

Draw fish, birds and other animals to complete the picture.

Use these words to label the pictures.
These are things for which we should be thankful.

pets	trees	my home	good food

home

food

pets

trees

I am also thankful for my famly and the moutis and the skiey and lief Jesus.

14

Lesson Four
God Makes Man

Use these words to complete the sentences.

father	love	obey	mother

Adam was the first _father_ .

Eve was the first _mother_ .

Mothers and fathers must love and _obey_ God.

Children must _bovey_ and obey their parents.

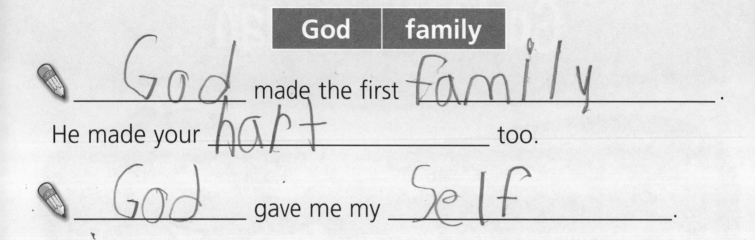

God | family

_____God_____ made the first _____family_____.

He made your _____hart_____ too.

_____God_____ gave me my _____self_____.

Color the family in the picture below.

God gives everyone work to do. There is work for mothers and fathers. There is work for little boys and girls. When we do our work, we should always do our best.

I work at _____.   I work at_____.

Use these words to complete the poem.

rest	might	right	best

I do my work

With all my *might* ;

God is pleased

When I do it *right* .

In all I do,

I do my *best* ,

After I work,

Then I can *rest* .

18

Lesson Six
Rules

Groups Need Rules

Write the correct numbers in the box beside each picture.

1. Raise hands for questions.
2. Line up for lunch.
3. Put trash in containers.
4. No running in halls.

Color the picture that shows a child obeying the rule about listening well in class.

Unit Two
God's Gift: Special Promises
Noah, Abraham, Jacob, And Joseph

Use these words to answer the questions.

| Noah | ark | flood |

What kind of boat did Noah make? _ark_

What did God bring on the earth? _flood_

Who was God's friend? _Noah_

Follow the dots to help finish the ark.

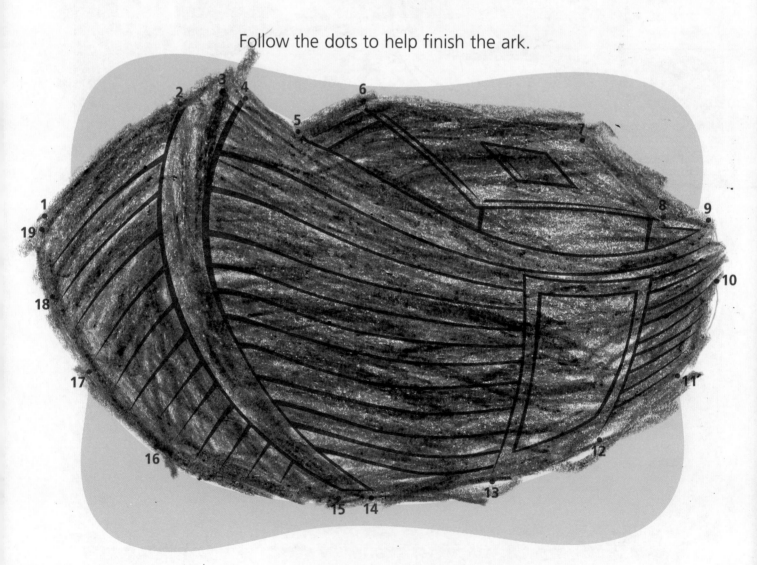

22

Write the correct numbers in the box beside each picture.

1. Noah prays and thanks God. **2.** The animals go into the ark.

3. Noah builds an ark. **4.** The Flood covers the earth.

Color the rainbow.

Yellow

Green

God's promises are a special gift.

Fill in the blanks by unscrambling the words.

🖊 God promised in Genesis 9:11 that He would _never_

again send a _flood_ to destroy the _earth_ .
                      oodlf   ernve / rahet

This is how Abraham lived. Connect the dots then color to complete the picture.

Use these words to answer the questions.

punished	blessed

God _blessed_ Abraham because he trusted God.

God _punished_ Lot because he chose selfishly.

Jacob Has A Dream

These words state the promise God gave Jacob in Genesis 28:15.
Write them in the correct order on the steps of the stairway going up.

| will | not | you | leave | I |

5. you

4. leave

3. not

2. will

1. I

God's way is wise. When we choose our way, we are foolish.
Under each picture write the word that describes the picture—
either "wise" or "foolish."

Lesson Ten
Joseph Becomes A Leader

Write "**Jacob**" or "**Joseph**" below each picture.

Jacob

Joseph

Who confessed his sin? Jacob

Who forgave his brothers? Joseph

Number the pictures from Joseph's life in the correct order.

Head of Potiphar's house

Coat of many colors

Family moves to Egypt

In prison

Sold as a slave

Giving out food in Egypt

Unit Three
God's Gift: Worship
The Stories Of Josiah And Joash

Draw the crown on Josiah's head to make him king.

Fill in the blanks below by unscrambling the words to learn what happened in 2 Chronicles 34:1-2.

Josiah was ___eight___ years old when he became
        gheit

___King___. He did what was _____ in
   kngi   tirgh

the eyes of the _____ and walked in God's _____.
                  droL   ysaw

33

Church is a gift from God.

Complete each sentence with one of these words.

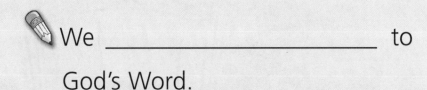

| pray | sing praises | listen |

We _____ to God's Word.

We _____ and give thanks.

We _____ _____ to God.

Josiah Reads God's Word

King Josiah promised to obey all the laws of the Lord.

Number the pictures in the right order.

The idols are broken.

God's law is found.

Josiah is the king.

God's house is fixed.

King Josiah made a promise Like This one. can you make iT Too?

Use these words to make for yourself the same promise David made in Psalm 119:11.

sin	Word	heart

Lord, I will hide your _____

in my _____ so that

I will not _____ against You.

Lesson Thirteen
Joash—The Boy Who Forgot God

When Joash grew up, he forgot to serve the Lord. We need to serve the Lord now and stay faithful for the rest of our lives.

Use these words to complete the promise.

life	right	Lord	eyes	days

My promise to God:

I will do _____ in the _____ of the _____ all the _____ of my _____.

_____
your name here

37

Do you serve idols or The True God?

In 1 Thessalonians 1:9, Paul says that he is glad to hear about people who turned to God from idols to serve the living and true God.

Circle the pictures that show how we worship the one true God.

Who am I?

Write the correct name below each picture.

Adam & Eve | Noah | Abraham | Jacob | Joseph | Josiah

Abraham

Jacob

Josiah

Noah

Adam Eve

Joseph

Unit Four
God's Gift: A Savior
The Stories Of Jesus

Luke 1-2

The Savior is Born!

An Angel Visits Mary

Mary's Gift From God

Use these words to complete the sentences.

angel	Jesus	joy	heart

Mary loved God with all her _heart_.

An _angel_ came to visit Mary.

Mary would have a baby named _Jesus_.

Mary sang a song of _joy_. Her baby would be God's Son.

Fill in the blanks with these three words from Luke 2:46-49.

name	God	holy

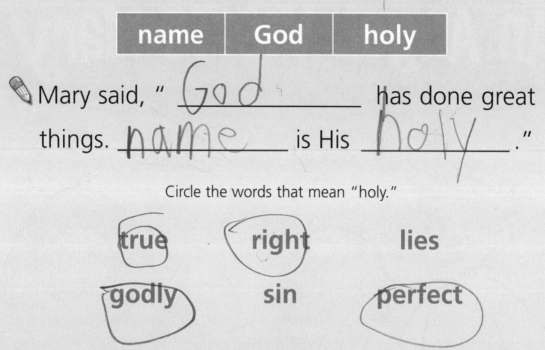

Mary said, " _God_ has done great things. _name_ is His _holy_ ."

Circle the words that mean "holy."

true   right   lies

godly   sin   perfect

Write the names of the three people to whom the angel appeared below the correct pictures.

Zacharias	Mary	Joseph

Lesson Fifteen
Jesus Is Born

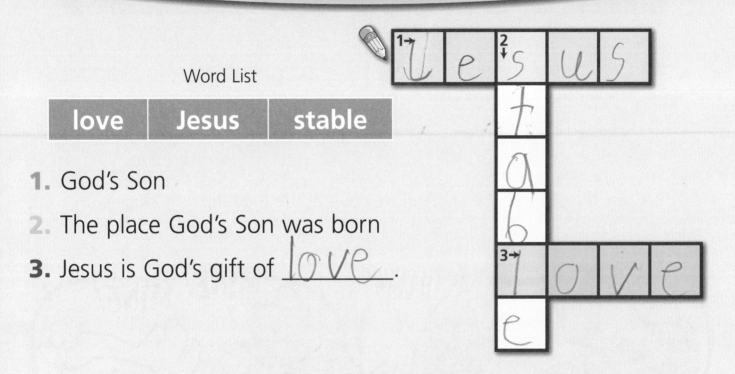

Word List

love	Jesus	stable

1. God's Son

2. The place God's Son was born

3. Jesus is God's gift of __love__.

Crossword answers:
1→ Jesus
2↓ stable
3→ love

Connect the dots and color to see where Mary placed Jesus after He was born.

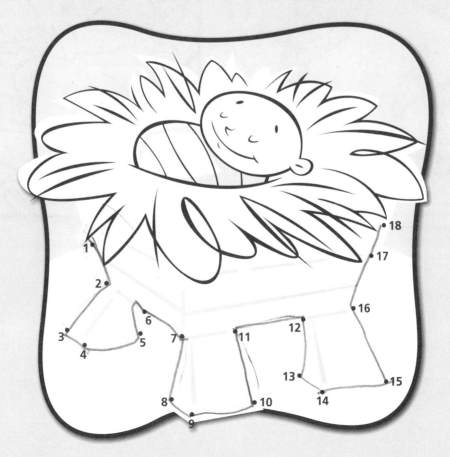

Use this code to complete the truth from Ephesians 4:32.

Code Box

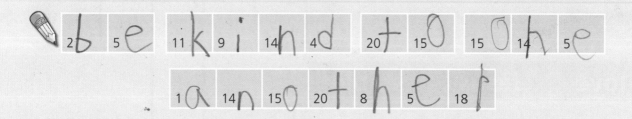

a	b	c	d	e	f	g	h	i	j	k	l	m
1	2	3	4	5	6	7	8	9	10	11	12	13

n	o	p	q	r	s	t	u	v	w	x	y	z
14	15	16	17	18	19	20	21	22	23	24	25	26

b e   k i n d   t o   o n e
2 5   11 9 14 4   20 15   15 14 5

a n o t h e r
1 14 15 20 8 5 18

Color the pictures, then circle the picture of the child showing kindness.

46

Color the picture by number.

Bethlehem is the city of David. Who does Luke 2:11 say was born in that city?

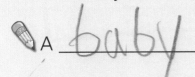 A baby who is Christ the Lord

Help the wise men use the Star of Bethlehem to find Jesus.

James 1:17 teaches us that every good __gift__ is from God.

Lesson Seventeen
The Boy Jesus

God wants us to grow up in many ways.

Write the numbers of the two items that apply to each picture in the boxes.

1 Read   **3** Praise God   **5** Go to church   **7** Write

2 Love   **4** Grow tall   **6** Grow strong   **8** Help others

Wisdom `1` `7`

Stature `6` `4`

Favor With Man `2` `8`

Favor With God `5` `3`

Learn To be Like Jesus.

Word List

 | obey |  | kind | work

Across:

1. Jesus liked to _____ in the carpenter shop.

4. Jesus liked to _____ what He had with others.

Down:

2. Jesus would always _____ His mother.

3. Jesus was good and _____ .

5. Jesus was a _____ to others.

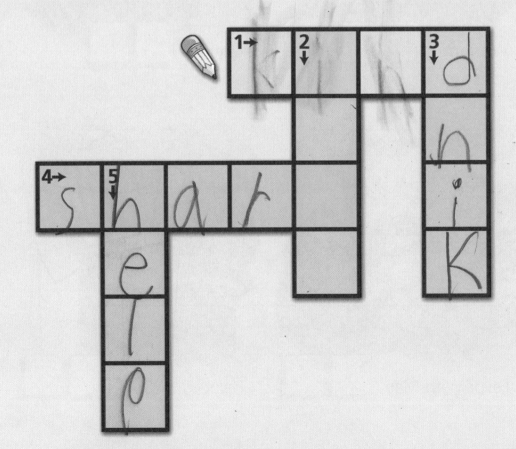

Draw a smile on the faces in front of the sentences that are right.
Draw a frown on the faces in front of the sentences that are wrong.

 SaTan is God's enemy.

 Jesus wanTed To obey SaTan.

 Jesus cannoT sin because He is God.

 Jesus did noT answer SaTan.

 The Word of God helps us fighT againsT SaTan.

How God used angels . . .

Use these words to fill in the blanks.

In special _____care_____

To tell Mary that _____birth_____ was going to be born

To tell the shepherds of Jesus' _____dreams_____

To _____Jesus_____ for Jesus (and also for us)

Lesson NineTeen
Jesus Calls His Disciples

Jesus wants us to learn from others. Where can we go to learn?

Use these words to complete the sentences.
Then draw lines to the pictures that match the sentences.

| church | home | school |

Eastwood Christian School

I learn from my parents at
home.

I learn to read from my teacher at
school.

I learn more about Jesus in
church.

A disciple Learns To be Like Jesus.

Word List

love	joy	kind	obey

obey
beoy

joy
yoj

love
olve

kind
nikd

Lesson Twenty
Jesus Loves Children

Draw a smile on the faces in front of the sentences that are right.
Draw a frown on the faces in front of the sentences that are wrong.

 The disciples were glad to see the children with Jesus.

 Jesus wanted the children to come to Him.

 The children were afraid of Jesus.

 Jesus told the children never to be afraid.

 Jesus wants us to obey and love one another.

Jesus' words show us how much he cared about children.
In Luke 18:16, what does Jesus command his disciples to do?

Let the little _children_ come to me.

Color those who Jesus loves.

Lesson Twenty-One
Jesus Feeds The 5,000

Number the pictures in the right order.

3

The disciples fed the people bread and fish.

1

"There is no food. We must send the people home."

4

There were 12 baskets of food left.

2

"I will share my lunch."

We must Learn To share what Jesus gives us.

What can boys and girls give To God?

Unscramble the words in the churches to fill in the blanks.

yots

I can share my _toys_ with friends.

lfse

I can give my _self_ when I help others.

chchru

I can bring offerings when I go to _church_.

rchose

I can do my _chose_ without being told.

In Matthew 14:25-27, what did the disciples think they saw on the water?

A goste

Who was it really? Jesus

What did Jesus say they should not do? to not be afraid

Who made the sea and wind quiet? Jesus

Color the picture to match the small colored one.

Use these words to fill in the blanks.

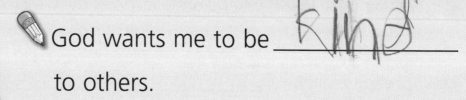

share courage kind wisdom

God wants me to be __kind__ to others.

Jesus gives us __courage__ so we do not have to be afraid.

God wants us to __share__ what we have.

When we learn, we have more __wisdom__.

Lesson Twenty-Three
Jesus Heals A Blind Man

Look up the verses and complete the quotations.

Jesus, *have mercy on me.*

(Mark 10:47)

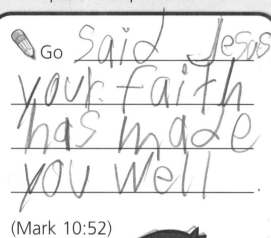

Go *said Jesus your faith has made you well*

(Mark 10:52)

These are some ways we can show thankfulness to God.
Use these words to label the pictures.

| giving | serving | thanking | singing |

_____

_____

Dear God, Thank You for _heping me make the rihgt diecinshs_

Love, _CULLEN DAVIS_

62

The Lost Sheep

Use these words to complete the sentences.
Then draw lines to the pictures that match the sentences.

shepherd	sheep	cares	lost

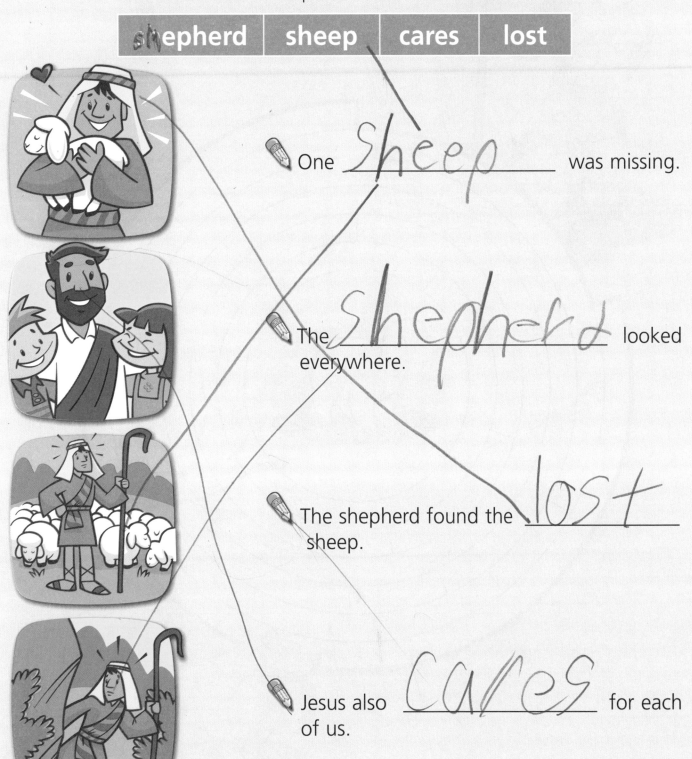

One _sheep_ was missing.

The _shepherd_ looked everywhere.

The shepherd found the _lost_ sheep.

Jesus also _cares_ for each of us.

HeLp The shepherd find The LOST sheep.

Jesus is The Good Shepherd.

Word List

sheep   lost   saved   Jesus   cares

Across:

1. One sheep was ___lost___.

3. ___Jesus___ loves each of His children.

5. The Good Shepherd ___cares___ for each one of His sheep.

Down:

2. The shepherd loved every ___sheep___.

4. Jesus calls each person to be ___saved___.

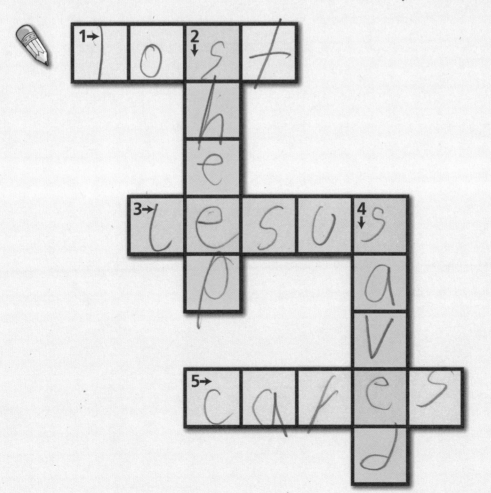

Jesus Is Crucified

Match the following questions with the pictures below.

_____ Who pretended to be Jesus' friend?

_____ Who took Jesus away?

_____ Who yelled, "Crucify Him!"?

_____ Who died on the cross for our sins?

_____ Who is Jesus?

A. Jesus

B. The People

C. God

D. Judas

E. Soldiers

God Sees Our Hearts.

Write the words in the correct column.

cheerful	proud	honest	wicked
good	joyful	foolish	fearful

RighT

✏ _____ heart

✏ _____ heart

✏ _____ heart

✏ _____ heart

Wrong

✏ _____ heart

✏ _____ heart

✏ _____ heart

✏ _____ heart

In 1 Samuel 16:7 we learn that the Lord looks at the _____.

Lesson Twenty-Six
Jesus Lives!

Draw a smile on the faces in front of the sentences that are right.
Draw a frown on the faces in front of the sentences that are wrong.

 Jesus did not know what would happen to Him.

 Jesus was in the tomb for three days.

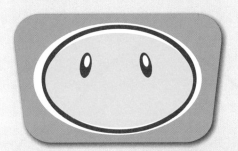 Jesus' promise came true. Jesus rose again.

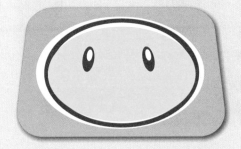 Jesus is God.

The Life Of Christ

Write the correct number in the box beside each picture.

1. Jesus cares for us.

2. Jesus rose again.

3. Jesus died on the cross.

4. God's Son was born.

OTTer PhoTography

FamiLY PorTraiTs
$10

Hannah Prays For A Son

Use these words to complete the puzzle.

Elkanah	Samuel	prayed	child	son	faith

1. Hannah wanted a _child_ (1 Samuel 1:11).

2. She _prayed_ to God (1 Samuel 1:10).

3. Her husband was _Elkanah_ (1 Samuel 1:8).

4. Hannah prayed for a _son_ (1 Samuel 1:11).

5. She named her son _Samuel_ (1 Samuel 1:20).

6. Hannah had _faith_ in God (1 Samuel 1:18).

Samuel was a special gift from God.
You are a special gift too.

Tell how God made you special by filling in the blanks on the mirror.

✎ I have _____ hair.

✎ I have _____ eyes.

✎ My birthday is _____.

✎ I have _____ brothers

and _____ sisters.

✎ I like to eat _____.

✎ My favorite game is _____

_____.

✎ Something very special about me is

_____

_____.

Begin with the S and circle every other letter.

Write the circled letters in the correct order to learn how Samuel answered God in 1 Samuel 3:10.

SPEAK FOR YOUR SERVANT LISTENS.

To Whom Does the Lord Want Us to Listen?

Use these words to complete the sentences.

Bible	pastor	parents	teacher

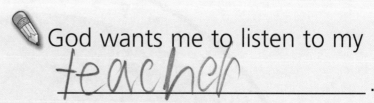 God wants me to listen to my _teacher_.

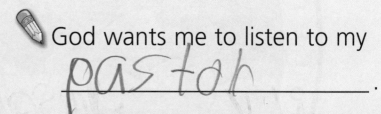 God wants me to listen to my _pastor_.

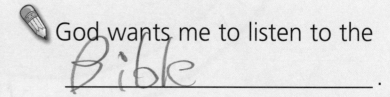 God wants me to listen to the _Bible_.

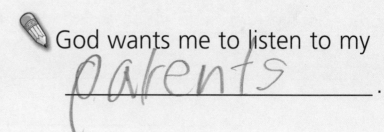 God wants me to listen to my _parents_.

Who am I?

Write the name of the correct person below each picture.

| Abraham | Hannah | Joseph | Mary | Jesus | Samuel |

Mary

Joseph

Samuel

Jesus

_____

Hannah

David Is Chosen As King

In your own words . . .

What is Samuel telling Jesse?

Go get David

What is Samuel telling David?

You will be the next king.

What was God's plan for David . . .

When he was young? Sheperd

When he became a man? King

What is God's plan for you now?

Use these words to label the pictures.

play	listen	read	work

🖊 *play*

🖊 *lisen*

🖊 *read the bed*

🖊 *warkly close*

🖊 I can show responsibility by *make the bed wash my close* .

82

Lesson Thirty
David And Goliath

Use these words to complete the sentences.

Goliath	God	David	stones	one

The shepherd boy who had courage to fight the giant was _David_.

David picked up five _stones_ for his sling.

He only had to use _one_ stone.

David killed the giant, _Goliath_.

David was not afraid because _God_ was with him.

Use this code to discover the truths about God in Isaiah 41:10.

= A   = E   = I   = O   = U

DOn't bE AfrAid; Only bElIEvE.

FEAr nOt, bEcAUsE I Am wIth yOU;

i Am yOUr GOd.

✏ Who alone can take away your fears? God

84

David And Jonathan

Word List

David	covenant	sword	love

Find 1 Samuel 18.

18:1 Jonathan loved **(3 down)** in the same way he loved himself.

18:3 Jonathan and David made a **(1 down)** because of their **(4 across)** for each other.

18:4 Jonathan gave David his **(2 across)** and robe to wear.

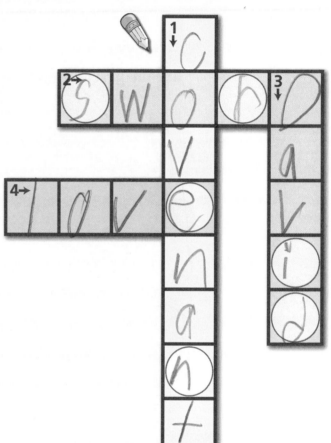

Unscramble the circled letters to complete the following sentence.

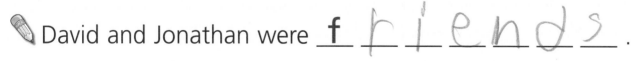

David and Jonathan were **f** r i e n d s .

Write the words in the box that tell how friends should act.

jealous   loving
rude   helpful
giving   unkind
kind   friendly

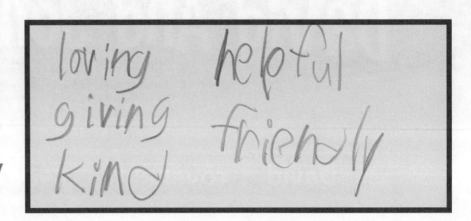

What other words can you think of that tell how friends should act? _____

_____

_____

God uses us in many ways.

Write the correct word to complete each statement.

| king | musician | friend | shepherd |

David was a...

friend

king

shepherd

musican

Write the correct letter in the box beside each picture.

A. "This is all I have left."   **B.** "Cook some bread."

C. "Thank you for helping me."   **D.** "Would you give me some food?"

Use these words to answer the questions.

| Elijah | the woman | God | the son |

🖊 Who had a son that died?_____

🖊 Whom did the woman tell about her son?_____

🖊 Who laid himself on the boy and cried out to God?_____

🖊 Who came back to life?_____

🖊 Who made the boy live again?_____

God answers prayer.

Each picture shows a time to pray. Tell when you can pray under each picture.

🖊 _____ 🖊 _____ 🖊 _____

🖊 I can also pray when _____

_____.

Lesson Thirty-Three
Elijah Prays To God

Draw a smile on the face if the answer is yes or a frown if the answer is no.

 Did Baal answer the prayers of the people?

 Did Elijah pray to the true God?

 Did Baal send fire down on the altar?

 Did God send fire down on Elijah's altar?

 Is there only one true God?

Draw the fire on Elijah's altar.

Complete the prayer with these words.

God	true	prayers

Dear God,

I thank You that You are the _____ God. There is

no _____ besides You who can hear our _____ .

Elijah Goes To Heaven

Acts 16:31 teaches that if we believe in the Lord Jesus, God will save us.

Choose the correct solution for reaching God from the words below and write it on the bridge that reaches to God.

Going To Church	Serving Others	Faith In Jesus

GOD

Obeying Your Parents

Saying Prayers

In order for me to be saved, what is . . .

 My Responsibility? _____

 God's Promise? _____

God's Forever Gift: Heaven

Use the code to discover what Jesus said in John 14:2.

a	b	c	d	e	f	g	h	i	j	k	l	m
1	2	3	4	5	6	7	8	9	10	11	12	13

n	o	p	q	r	s	t	u	v	w	x	y	z
14	15	16	17	18	19	20	21	22	23	24	25	26

___ ___ ___ ___ ___ ___ ___ ___   ___ ___
 9   1   13   7 15   9 14   7   20 15

___ ___ ___ ___ ___ ___ ___   ___
16 18   5   16   1 18   5   1

___ ___ ___ ___ ___ ___ ___ ___   ___ ___ ___.
16 12   1   3   5   6 15 18   25 15 21

96

Write the name of the correct person below each picture.

David	Josiah	Samuel	Jesus	Noah	Elijah

_____

_____

_____

_____

_____

_____

God's Gift Of Forgiveness For Christians

In 1 John 1:9, we learn that if we confess our sins, we can trust God to forgive us.

Write what we should do in the spaces below.

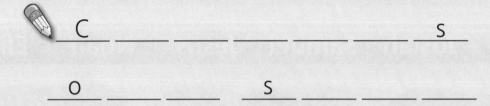

__ C __ __ __ __ __ __ __ s __

__ o __ __ __ s __ __ __ __ __

Write what God promises to do in the spaces below.

__ F __ __ __ __ g __ __ __ __ __ __ u __

Enjoying God's Gifts Scripture Memorization Report Sheet

Name: _____ Grade: _____ Teacher: _____

Week	Scripture	Due Date	Parent's Signature
1	Gen. 1:1		
2	Gen. 1:31a		
3	Eph. 6:1		
4	Eph. 6:2		
5	Eph. 6:1-2		
6	Eph. 6:1-3		
7	Gen. 9:11c		
8	Gen. 12:2a		
9	Gen. 28:15b		
10	**Review**		
11	Prov. 3:5		
12	Prov. 3:6		
13	**Prov. 3:5-6**		
14	Luke 1:49		
15	Luke 2:7		
16	Luke 2:11		
17	Luke 2:52		
18	**Review**		
19	Matt. 4:19		
20	Luke 18:16		
21	Eph. 4:32		
22	Matt. 14:27b		
23	Mark 10:52a		
24	John 10:11		
25	John 3:16		
26	**Review**		
27	Psalm 23:1		
28	Psalm 23:2		
29	Psalm 23:3		
30	**Psalm 23:1-3**		
31	Psalm 23:4		
32	Psalm 23:5		
33	Psalm 23:6		
34	**Psalm 23:4-6**		
35	**Psalm 23:1-6**		